Pressure, resistance, empowerment:
Young women and the negotiation of safer sex

Women, Risk, and AIDS Project

Young women, sexuality and the limitation of AIDS

The initial focus on high risk groups in the AIDS epidemic led to women being considered to be at little risk from HIV infection and AIDS. Growing evidence has called this focus into question, and indicated that the spread of AIDS is a matter of high risk practices rather than group membership. The potential role of young women in this process has not been fully explored.

The WRAP investigation is exploring the sexual practices, beliefs and understanding of young women. Two groups in inner city areas of London and Manchester are being studied, using a range of research methods. The study is producing a detailed description and analysis of what young women know about sexuality and about AIDS; the ideas which they have about risk, danger and control in sexual encounters; how they behave sexually; why they behave as they do, and what factors are likely to constrain or to encourage change in their behaviour.

The practical application of the study is directly relevant to the containment of the AIDS epidemic. The information gathered is also relevant to changing other aspects of health care related to women's sexual behaviour and will generate practical recommendations which will have policy implications in the field of health, sex and AIDS education.

The WRAP team

Janet Holland,	*Senior Research Lecturer, Institute of Education, London*
Caroline Ramazanoglu,	*Senior Lecturer, Goldsmiths College, London*
Sue Scott,	*Lecturer, University of Manchester*
Sue Sharpe,	*Consultant Researcher, London*
Rachel Thomson,	*Consultant Researcher, London*

Descriptions of the WRAP Papers may be found at the back of this book.

Pressure, resistance, empowerment:
Young women and the negotiation of safer sex

Janet Holland, Caroline Ramazanoglu, Sue Scott, Sue Sharpe, and Rachel Thomson

WRAP PAPER 6

the Tufnell Press, London

the Tufnell Press,
47 Dalmeny Road,
London, N7 0DY

First published June 1991
Reprinted November 1993

British Library Cataloguing-in-Publication Data
A catalogue record for this book is
available from the British Library

ISBN 1-872767-75-3

Printed in England by Instant Print West One, London.

Contents

Introduction

Knowledge of the risks of the sexual transmission of HIV among young heterosexuals is spreading, but controlling sexual safety can be problematic for young women if they play subordinate roles in sexual encounters. Once people have been given information on how HIV can be transmitted sexually, and advice on safer sex, they still have to make sense of what they have learned. They have to consider whether what they know has any bearing on their own lives, and how, when or whether to put this knowledge into practice. Rates of teenage pregnancy and rising rates of sexually transmitted diseases indicate that, whatever women's intentions, risky sexual practices are still widespread among young heterosexuals (OPCS 1988, Estaugh and Wheatley 1990).

Previous research in medical sociology indicates that possession of knowledge has no necessary connection with changes in risk-taking behaviour (Azjen and Fishbein 1980; Hanson et al. 1987). Knowledge of risk has to be incorporated into people's understandings of their own situations to bring about any interest in change, and this involves people in an active process of reflection (Raven and Litman-Adizes 1986; Hunt and Macleod 1987). Such knowledge as does exist at present about the behaviour of heterosexuals indicates little change to safer sexual behaviour, apart from a slightly increased use of condoms (*AIDS Newsletter* 10.12.1990). Department of Health figures in January 1991 show that while new cases of seropositivity in homosexual and bisexual men fell between 1989 and the end of 1990, new cases of seropositive heterosexual men and women increased over the same period. Current projections show the proportion of seropositive women to men is likely to increase steadily (OPCS 1991).

We have argued previously (Holland *et al.* 1991a) that variations in levels of power and autonomy in the negotiation of sexual encounters can contribute to unsafe sexual behaviour. Young women have to cope with conflicting social pressures in organising their sexual behaviour and the outcomes can be both positive and negative. The extent to which young heterosexual women define sex in terms of love, romance and relationships with men leads to a widespread acceptance of sexual practices being defined in terms of men's needs. This gives men, whether wittingly or not, considerable power over young women's sexual practices. The tragedy of the AIDS epidemic has now given urgency to questions about the ways in which safer sexual practices can be promoted within gendered social relationships.

Women who want to ensure their own sexual safety have to be socially assertive and so to be prepared to challenge, to some extent at least, the conventions of femininity (Holland *et al.* 1991a). Those who value their control of sexuality have to be prepared to lose the valued social relationship with a sexual partner or potential partner (see also Gross and Bellew-Smith 1983). Young women who assert their own needs have to negotiate sexual relationships with men which resist the commonsense of masculine and feminine sexuality. The understanding of sexual risk-taking by young women and the promotion of safer sex for young heterosexuals will depend on how we can make connections between the sexual pressures on young women, their resistance to these pressures and their personal empowerment in managing their own lives.

In this paper, we reflect on the sexual politics of safer sex by considering the ways in which the empowerment of young women can be conceptualised in sexual encounters. These related themes of pressure, resistance and empowerment are developed through analysis of data from the *Women, Risk and AIDS Project's* interviews with 150 young women in London and Manchester.[1] From these young women's accounts of their sexual relationships, we consider the question of how far their needs for sexual safety are compromised by pressures to service men's needs in sexual relationships, and how far they subordinate their own sexual safety to their expectations of men's needs and desires. We argue that for a young woman to negotiate safe sex in a heterosexual relationship she has to be empowered both to develop a positive conception of feminine sexuality and to be able to put this positive conception into practice. We argue below that empowerment at one level does not necessarily entail empowerment at another.

The context of empowerment - pressures from men in sexual encounters

Most of the young women's accounts of their first sexual experiences are either negative or indicate limited satisfaction. When young women, often under the age of consent, begin to engage in sexual relationships and to test out their sexual identities, they do not initially have direct personal experience to draw on and much that they need to know is hidden from them.[2] They have to make sense of information from different sources - childhood experiences, schools, youth workers, parents and siblings, peers, the mass media - which often give them contradictory messages (Thompson 1984). Since there is no overriding conception of a positive and enjoyable female sexuality in which women are both acceptably feminine and in control of their sexuality, they have to relate the ideas about love, romance and femininity which they bring to their sexual relationships, to their initial experiences with men.

Nearly a quarter of the sample (thirty five young women out of one hundred and fifty) had had unwanted sexual intercourse in response to pressure from men.[3] These pressures varied from mild insistence on giving way to intercourse, or to intercourse on his terms, to threats, physical assault, child abuse and rape. Young women in their interviews gave accounts of situations in which various forms of violence had played a part and in which they have had to make sense of the extent to which they could exercise control over their own sexuality. Even where women had not been directly pressured by men, or were not sexually active, the extent to which male pressure is incorporated into the conventions of 'normal' heterosexuality provides the cultural context within which young women have to negotiate their own safety (Hanmer and Maynard 1987; Kelly 1988; Stanko 1985). Health promotion strategies then need to take this context of pressure into account.

Safer sex, heterosexuality and the empowerment of young women

In the health promotion literature there is little or no account of gendered power relations which could challenge conceptions of heterosexual sex as natural. There has been a tendency for the Health Education Authority and other producers of educational materials to focus on a narrow conception of heterosexuality which is drawn in a male image. The senior programme officer for the HEA's Sexual Health Programme has commented:

'... our advertising directed at heterosexuals has necessarily concentrated on the need for protected penetrative sex.' (Christophers 1990:6)

It is significant that while the AIDS crisis has opened up the possibility of validating non-penetrative sexual practices, and thus of a move towards less male-centred understandings of heterosexuality (Coward 1987), the dominant definition of safer sex has focused on how to reduce the risks attached to vaginal penetration. The success of this definition can be illustrated by the fact that the majority of our respondents equated safer sex simply and directly with condom use. Heterosexual sexuality continues to be closely tied at the level of ideology to procreation; any move towards separating sex from reproduction leads to anxiety and outrage as is evidenced by emotional reactions to the possibility of 'virgin births', in which women can be artificially inseminated without the need ever to have had a sexual relationship with a man (Rumbold 1991).

Thinking about empowerment in relation to safer sex is constrained by existing assumptions and categories of thought which define heterosexual sex in terms of a dominant masculinity. This conception of heterosexuality tends to perceive safe sex as the responsibility of individual men and women who are free to make rational choices for their own protection. The logical consequence of this rational choice model of sexual action has been to direct sex education towards individuals in order to inform their choices (Jessop and Thorogood 1989).[4] It leaves as unproblematic the conception of sex as a set of acts leading to penetration and male orgasm. In this conception of sex, safety becomes reduced to the punctual intervention of the condom (Freeman and Scott). Young women's knowledge of and access to contraception may effectively structure what is thought of as 'sex'. The definition of safer sex in terms of effective condom use reinforces, through practice, the central place of male erection and orgasm in sexual encounters. To plan to protect oneself with a condom presupposes something to put it on.[5] The use of condoms should then be seen not as a neutral and rational response to HIV prevention, but as a compromise with existing patriarchal ideology and practices. The extent to which the nature of heterosexuality is assumed leaves, as Tamsin Wilton has put it, 'heterosexual man as the great undiscussed' (Wilton 1990).

Mukesh Kapila suggests that:

'In the long term, a sexually healthy population requires the creation of a social climate which enables individuals to relate

> to each other in mutually respectful relationships. Only then will individual-directed education be acceptable. ... we can't expect all individuals to solve problems which really belong in a wider context.' (Williams 1990:4)

The point which Kapila overlooks is that heterosexual relationships do not take place between socially equivalent individuals but between gendered persons. The practical problems of how 'mutually respectful relationships' can emerge from the inequalities of gender have still to be addressed. The conception of safer sex as a matter of individual choice and responsibility separates it from debates about citizenship which could place sexual safety on a public and collective agenda alongside such issues as child abuse, violence against women and new reproductive technologies. It is not yet the case that the promotion of safer sex has been wholly medicalised, rather it is currently a contested terrain in which safer heterosexual identities can be negotiated in struggle against the idea of natural and dominant male sexuality.

Our data have implications for a critical evaluation of the 'solutions' to HIV/AIDS which have come from state agencies and biomedicine. The perceived need for an absolute guide to safety has rendered health promotion dependent on imperfect medical knowledge about the different kinds of risks. The hidden assumption in many safer sex guidelines (Setters 1988) is that decisions about risk in relation to HIV are governed by rationality, rather than by the multifaceted and often contradictory pressures of everyday life.

If we want to think of women as able to struggle against the pressures of patriarchal societies, by finding their own sources of power, we need to be specific as to what these sources could be. While some young women are relatively advantaged by their class background, their level of education or their ethnicity, there is no clear material or gendered base for sexual empowerment. It is easy to talk of how to empower young women so as to make sex safer or more pleasurable, it is harder to specify what exactly is meant by empowerment in relation to safer sex. There is a tension here between ideas of empowerment as individual assertiveness or individual choices, and a more collective notion of empowerment as a challenge to dominant masculinity. Whereas the exercise of male power is taken to be the subordination and control of women by men, we do not take women's empowerment to be the subordination of men.

Envisaging empowerment for young women means defining the power relations which could be changed and defining how these relationships can be transformed. In the context of sexual encounters, empowering women could mean: not engaging in sexual activity; not engaging in sexual activity without informed consent; getting men to consent to safer practices; negotiating sexual practices which are pleasurable to women as well as to men.

The method of analysis

In order to clarify what empowerment means in practice, we have used the technique of systemic networks in the analysis of our data.[6] The use of the network allows us to organise our data in terms of a range of sources of pressure from men and empowerment of young women. This gives us a theoretical map of the pressures and responses which impinge on young women's sexuality. The *empowerment network* which we have used for this paper is laid out in the Appendix, and the young women's accounts which follow have been analysed using the categories in this network. For the purposes of this paper, we consider only the key categories to show, through young women's accounts, how empowerment can be understood as a process of struggle, rather than as a static category of knowledge or practice.

In coding and analysing the interview transcripts in terms of this network, we drew on three levels of conceptualisation: the terms and meanings used by the young women and explicit in the data; the interviewer's fieldnotes made after the interview, which entail some interpretation of meanings in the interview; team members' discussion, interpretation and coding of these data in the light of feminist and sociological theory.[7] These levels of interpretation helped us to analyse accounts of pressure and empowerment where the researchers' interpretation differed from that of the young woman's. For example where a young woman defined herself as empowered, and the researchers did not categorise her in this way. The interaction of these levels of interpretation is built into the categories of the network.

For the purposes of this paper we have drawn on a sub-set of twenty six young women whose accounts identified them as relatively empowered in negotiations around sexual intercourse and sexual relationships. Of these, twenty two were or had been sexually active, and eleven of these, that is half of those who were sexually active, had had pressured sexual experiences in the form of sexual abuse as children, rape or unwanted sexual intercourse under threat or other pressure from men. In comparison with the sample as a whole this sub-set of 26 was very slightly biased towards the middle class and the older age groups. They had, on average, had slightly more casual sexual partners than the sample as a whole. Fifteen had had unprotected sex which had put them at potential risk of HIV infection, and eight had had unprotected sex which put them at risk of pregnancy, but this was a lower rate of unsafe sex than that of the sample as a whole. In other respects they did not differ significantly from the rest of the sample.

The material for this paper has been informed by a cross-cut analysis of these 26 empowered young women, looking at specific categories in this sub-set of cases. We do not present these data here but, in order to clarify the main points of our analysis, we have picked out the cases of five young women whose accounts illustrate different aspects of the contradictory processes of empowerment.

Empowerment as process

The empowerment network is not conceptualised as a set of static categories to which young women can be assigned, but as an attempt to capture the processes and possibilities of women's attempts to gain control of their sexuality. The empowerment of young women in negotiating safer sexual encounters can never simply be achieved but must be constantly struggled for.

The strategies for safer sex which young women bring to their sexual relationships help to shape the ways in which they plan sexual relationships and sexual practices. Their initial experiences then have to be made sense of in terms of the actual outcomes of sexual encounters, which may differ considerably from their intentions. Making sense of this gap can affect how empowered they may be in future relationships.

Since knowledge, intentions and control of situations in practice are not necessarily congruent, we have conceptualised young women's behaviour in terms of two levels. The *intellectual level* is that of the knowledge, expectations and intentions they bring to an encounter. The *experiential level* is the level of their sexual practice. The relationship between the intellectual and the experiential is never static, but develops and changes over time, as young women try to bring expectations and control of sexual situations more closely together. While empowerment always depends on gaining men's consent to women's definitions of the terms of sexual encounters, effective strategies for safer sex do not seem possible without some congruence between the intellectual and the experiential levels of empowerment.

Central to our understanding of empowerment is a third concept, that of a *transitional level* in the network. Since the empowerment of young women in sexual encounters is unstable and struggled over, the transitional category indicates that women may be empowered to the extent of controlling sexual encounters in some situations or with some partners, but not in others or with subsequent partners. The context-specific empowerment gives us a transitional rather than a static category. This notion of transition is an attempt to identify situations in which there is a mismatch between young women's intellectual empowerment and their capacity to put their intentions of controlling their sexuality into practice.

Young women can move in or out of this category in a process of interaction between intellectual and experiential levels of empowerment, with different outcomes in different sexual encounters, or over time. The additional category in the network of the combined *intellectual/experiential* level is a further attempt to grasp the process.

Five case studies

Intellectual empowerment

The problems of trying to classify young women according to their state of empowerment is illustrated by the category of intellectual empowerment. Both negative and positive sexual experiences can lead to empowerment in the form of self-awareness or knowledge based on the broader implications of sexual politics. But empowerment at the intellectual level is not sufficient to ensure safer sex. Young women who are empowered at this level may have sexual experiences which they are not able to control or resist, pushing them back into the transitional category where they have to struggle to gain ground that had been attained only at an intellectual level.

A number of young women expressed powerful intentions in their interviews. That is they gave accounts of their understanding of the risks of sexual encounters, and of their intentions in future sexual encounters. It was not possible in a single interview to follow up these intentions, but in those cases where young women reported retrospectively on their intentions and subsequent experiences the problems of putting intentions into practice were discussed. This came out clearly in cases where women understood the risks of unprotected sexual intercourse and intended to use condoms for their own safety, but in practice did not do so (Holland et al. 1991a). A 20% sub-sample of young women have been interviewed for a second time and in Nicky's case, the problems of treating intellectual empowerment as a static category can be seen in her account of her experiences between her first and second interviews.

Nicky[8]

Nicky was an attractive, confident young woman, not sexually active at our first interview, but very clear as to what her requirements would be of a partner. She was both very knowledgeable and concerned about HIV and AIDS and, when asked if she would take precautions in that respect if she were to have a sexual relationship, she asserted:

> A: Yeah, well if I wouldn't, then I wouldn't be in a relationship with them - I wouldn't if they couldn't accept that. It's just mindless not be aware of the risks and prepared to lessen them now.

Nicky can be regarded as intellectually empowered on several grounds: family background and support; personal conviction and self awareness; the ideology and practice of feminism and sexual politics. But the limitations of intellectual empowerment were shown in the second interview, which illustrated the processes involved in gaining and attempting to retain empowerment. Nicky had by then had three sexual relationships, and although she had mostly been able to uphold her insistence on safer sex, she had had unprotected sex on a number of occasions. She described her first experience of sex as good, although she was drunk at the time and unprotected. She took the morning after pill. After this it was usually condoms, "nasty little things, a bit revolting really, but worth it". This first boyfriend had been violent, although she presents this as shared violence despite some voiced doubts:

> A: We used to beat each other up quite frequently, every other day. - It does sound really bizarre and horrible, but it was quite enjoyable in a funny sort of way. - We both used to call a truce before we did any real damage. I have got bruises. I had bruises for the entire [time of the relationship].

> A: I think if I'd have wanted to stop it, I would have done. I remember thinking, "this is really strange". But I didn't - I'm not a violent person, I never fight. It seemed almost that he needed - he needed that, and in a way when he needed that, I went along with it.

The fights usually ended in sex, although the sex "was always him. It was for him. It wasn't really for me. He - he used to, you know, just get on with it really". After this sexual relationship finished, in a rather complicated fashion, the boyfriend visited her and effectively raped her, by forcing her to have sex which she did not want - she felt used and abused but could not stop him. She thought he had interpreted the event differently from her, since he had a notion of their relationship as one in which they could not control themselves. She had a scare about pregnancy at this point.

The second relationship "was actually completely sexual. I mean, I was going out with him for four months, and I never once saw him in daylight", but the sex was a lot better. This particular relationship demonstrated elements of the 'male model of sexuality', since she saw their mutual interest as being in a non-committed, non-involved sexual relationship, in which they could each have other partners. It ended when the young man went abroad. She subsequently embarked on what she took to be a serious relationship, only to be dropped by the young man without warning or explanation.

The start of Nicky's sexual relationships illustrated the movement from intellectual empowerment to sexual experiences in which it was difficult to maintain that power. In some respects she did, in that she was usually, although clearly not always, able to practice safer sex. She maintained a stance of equality in relationships, taking the first sexual partner with her to the clinic to get the morning after pill, but in many respects she was vulnerable and even abused, unable to stop unprotected sex being physically forced upon her, unable to protect herself emotionally from being abandoned by a sexual partner. "Mug, mug", was her own comment on herself.

The struggle for empowerment - the male model

While a number of young women gave accounts of their assertiveness in relation to men, much of this behaviour was not empowering in practice. The male model stresses the freedom of the individual to engage in sexual relationships without personal obligation. This disguises inequalities of power and control in sexual relationships with a liberal discourse of personal choice. It is an attractive model of sexual empowerment for young women who are trying to take control of their own lives and are resisting a passive model of female sexuality, but it does not allow women to recognise or challenge male power.

The case which follows is of a young woman who is consciously trying to be sexually empowered, to operate sexually on an equal basis with men. However the way in which she conceives her empowerment is contradicted by her involvement in relationships where her sexual practice puts her at risk.

Angela

At the time of her interview Angela was eighteen years old. She was supposed to be attending college, had her own car and, in her words was, "totally going out in search of a good time". She had recently become involved in a punk scene based on a council estate in which drug use, including intravenous drug use, was common. She was four weeks into a relationship with Tony who she described as, "a bit of a drop out". For Angela, who had had a conventional middle class upbringing, this new life was challenging and exciting. She perceived herself as empowered by the choices she was making as part of her personal growth.

A: I am not trying to shock them [parents and old friends] but I'm just trying to find myself and find out what sort of person I really am. I just do what I want to do because I don't want to get older and wish I had done that when I was younger. I intend doing it when I am younger so I have got no regrets.

Her aspirations in terms of sexual relationships show a similar confidence and a desire to engage on equal terms with men, challenging conventional models of feminine behaviour.

A: I just get carried away. I believe in equality, like a woman has a need as much as a man, and I think at the time, "Oh yes, sod it". A fellow is allowed to get a pat on the back and a drink bought them.

This male model of sexual assertiveness includes a belief in her right to sexual pleasure.

A: If a man is going with a woman he gets his pleasure, and then it's wrong that a lot of lads don't bother so much about the woman. Sort of like a quick grope then in and out sort of thing and I hate that. I think you have got to have consideration. With this lad - that I think was one of the most pleasurable experiences I ever had. But I think it is pretty important to a woman, we're entitled to it.

However this assertiveness, which can be conceived as intellectual empowerment, is experienced in a rather contradictory way. First she is attracted to men who will be a challenge to her, including men who will have power over her. She commented on a previous partner:

A: I hate weak men. He would do anything [I wanted him to] and I hate that. So I want someone who will keep me in my place.

Despite her intellectual empowerment, in her sexual practice she does not necessarily find herself able to act according to her intentions or to control sexual situations.

A: Sometimes you feel dead guilty when you are with a lad and [have] not tried to get him turned on and you feel it hard and pressed against your leg, and you're thinking "Oh shit, I didn't want that to happen at all". When I was younger I used to think I'll just let him, because I didn't want to be known as a prick tease.

In practice she experiences vulnerability.

A: I think I've got a bit of a muddle up somewhere along the line, because I interpret sex as feeling - well, if I feel unwanted and then I sleep with him then it makes me feel wanted. I was thinking last night and saying to him 'I've gone wrong somewhere' because I shouldn't have to do that.

Angela first had intercourse at fifteen. Initially she relied on occasional condom use combined with taking chances. Her best friend who relied purely on luck became pregnant and eventually had an abortion. This event provided an opportunity for Angela to reflect on her own behaviour. Making a decision to go on the pill, despite fear of her mother finding out can be seen as an empowering practice on the young woman's part and part of her growing assertiveness.

Although she had practised safe sex episodically in the past by using condoms, once she was using the pill she had to think more deliberately about risk-taking in sexual encounters. When asked about her intentions in relation to the practice of safe sex she recognised this.

A: If I met a lad who I didn't know anything about, I wouldn't think, well I'm on the pill and that will do, I think I would use a condom.

However subsequent discussion of her present relationship revealed putting safe sex into practice to be rather more problematic.

A: Tony doesn't really like using them. That used to annoy me, the fact that he knew we were going out and that we would probably end up [having sex without a condom].

Although she felt that asking a man to use a condom as a contraceptive was acceptable, citing fear of HIV as a reason was less easy.

A: I think that they would probably be dead insulted...I would take it personally, I would feel insulted.

The pill allows women to engage with men sexually without depending on them for contraception. Being on the pill allows women to meet men's needs without challenging the power dimension of the sexual situation. If a woman asks a man to use a condom when she is already on the pill, this alters the balance of the relationship by bringing into question the nature of the relationship and recognising the independent rights of both of those involved.

Angela's interview indicated the vulnerability of her position with Tony. Having said that she felt that AIDS only affected so called 'risk groups', she went on to reveal that Tony has not only been injecting intravenously for two years but, at times, sharing needles, and that they do not have safe sex. Despite her intention of remaining in control of her sexual practice her empowerment at the experiential level is undermined by the complicated issues of trust and commitment in this relationship.

> A: he always goes on about I don't trust him but when it comes down to it I think I do trust him, like I know he wouldn't go with anyone else, because he is a sort of one woman man, whereas I am like not a one man woman.

Angela's use of the contraceptive pill can be interpreted in terms of a male model of sexual empowerment. This model can be intellectually empowering, but is not empowering at the experiential level. The contradiction between the theory and practice of sexual empowerment is sharply focused by the risks she takes in having unsafe sex with Tony. Angela copes with these contradictions between intention and practice by distancing herself from the risks of HIV.

> A: I don't know anyone who has got AIDS so it's not too hard to forget about it.

Context-specific empowerment - the constraints on experiential empowerment

Sarah

Unlike Angela, Sarah was having safe sex at the time of her interview, in the sense that she was in a supposedly monogamous relationship and both she and her boyfriend had been tested for HIV before the relationship became sexual. This situation was initiated by Sarah in that she felt herself to have been at risk in previous relationships and had suggested the tests. She indicates a process of self reflection from which self awareness develops, leading to a need to take control of her sexuality; a process which we can understand as intellectual empowerment. However, as she herself points out, such empowerment does not change the social world.

> A: ... we have all these things on paper, all these theories where we say 'yes, we do this' but when it comes down to it would we do it? Have we done it? I think it takes quite a long time to develop. You can't just suddenly discover things and say "yes I will behave like that in future", you can't do that, you have to work towards it.

Sarah has managed to control and order events in such a way that she does feel in control of her present sexual relationship, but she acknowledges that she could be vulnerable again in the future:

> A: I was telling myself, if this relationship comes to an end, I'm never falling in the same trap as before, I'll make sure that I won't. - I'm more than fifty per cent confident that I won't, but not a full hundred per cent.

The story which Sarah told in the interview is marked by a recognition of her powerlessness and vulnerability in previous relationships and a dissatisfaction with the quality of those relationships. The trauma of an unplanned pregnancy, subsequent abortion and a cervical cancer scare appears to have acted as a catalyst enabling her to redefine her sexual behaviour and identity. However her explanation of this change is somewhat contradictory. On one hand she employs the restrictive discourse of post-AIDS morality to condemn the kind of sexual relationship and the model of sexual morality that she was previously involved in:

> A: You see the adverts on the media all the time telling you that it is bad to have so many sexual partners and this is why you have got all these increases - AIDS, and this is why there's an increase in cervical cancer in people under 25 and all this. - I think at the beginning I was thinking that it was normal, then I suddenly had this backlash when I thought it was a really bad thing that I had done by sleeping with these people.

On the other hand, we find that her rejection of this male model of sexual empowerment is rooted in her recognition of her own experience of powerlessness within such relationships. Her argument focuses upon a critical interpretation of the concept of choice:

> A: I thought it was that you had more choice, but I really wasn't having any choice in the matter. It's like the whole thing of the sixties, that sex is free for all. More of it available for more men, there is no risk in it. At the time I hadn't realised that was the case, that you had to decide, not just go along with it because it seems to be alright.

This growing awareness of her own powerlessness to decide and control the shape of her sexual relationships is reflected in her recollections of past behaviour.

> A: It wasn't that I wanted to take control over the other person, I just wanted to take an active part - I wasn't - I would be constantly doing things I didn't want to, and afterwards I would be chastising myself - I didn't realise why, but if there was someone there who would say, "yes, come out with me", I could say, "no". But then if there was some physical contact then I couldn't say no. - It took me a long time to work out these were the situations where I had a lack of power.

Available models of appropriate 'feminine' sexuality which value passivity place young women at a particular disadvantage, when they are engaging with men on the basis of a male-defined model of sexual empowerment and sexual norms.

> A: there was one particular relationship where I was sleeping with someone and I thought I was having a relationship, but they didn't know that they were having a relationship. Like that type of thing. It kept getting worse.

> A: I let myself get into a situation where I wasn't in control. I'm never doing it again. I'm going to sort it all out now for good.

For Sarah, making an active decision to enter a new relationship was an expression of self awareness and in itself a strategy of intellectual empowerment.

A: I also didn't start seeing him for a long time you know for - it was just after I had had an abortion and things like that. I didn't want to see anybody, and I didn't want to just fall into the thing you know, "if he likes me it will do, it doesn't matter, you know, what you feel", so I left it for a long time, about four months or something and didn't see him, and I actually decided to go into the relationship, not just sort of went along with it, I decided, and it is an active decision-making relationship instead of just jogging along.

The degree of control and responsibility which women exercise within sexual relationships has always been structured by their fears of pregnancy. The process of empowerment is structured in part by their experiences of and attitudes towards these contraceptive responsibilities. The additional necessity of safe sex, be it condom use, non-penetrative sex and/or monogamy, has further complicated this. Empowerment cannot simply be equated with safe sex. For Sarah, deciding to stop taking the pill was initially a positive and empowering decision.

A: I had decided that I did not want to take the pill, because I didn't see why I should take something internally and mess up my body when he could use a condom.

But condom use is problematic in that it necessitates a direct confrontation with male power within a sensitive and often non-verbal context.

A: I mean it is alright to think in advance - to use a condom all the time, but when it comes down to it either you won't or maybe you will. And that is what happened then - I didn't. It was a complete mistake, so I decided I would never let it happen again. ... because with a condom it is still your responsibility in a way, but then you are not wholly in control of it.

For these reasons Sarah returned to using the pill: "I would rather rely on myself than anyone else". Both she and her boyfriend had an HIV test and Sarah takes their relationship to be monogamous.

Sarah's account indicates some of the complexity of bringing intellectual and experiential levels of empowerment together. While clearly intellectually empowered she recognised situations where she could be at risk despite understanding and awareness. For Sarah, to ensure that she is in sexual relationships in which she can exercise control, she would have to be experientially empowered in a more stable way than she indicated in her interview. This does not mean being confident that she can always take control, or that she could manage safe sex in any sexual situation. Rather it entails recognising situations where she can be both intellectually and experientially empowered and avoiding situations within which she would be vulnerable.

Context-specific empowerment is a transitional and unstable category. This form of empowerment can lead to safer sex, for example, through lying to a partner about being on the pill and using condoms as well, or as Sarah did, having an HIV test and then maintaining a monogamous relationship. It remains a limited form of empowerment since though women may control particular situations they do so without seriously confronting male power, and so their strategies for safer sex may not always work.

Intellectual/experiential empowerment

Sharon

Sharon's sexual career had been a particularly negative and pressured set of experiences. Her account illustrates a painful process of developing self-knowledge and a conscious attempt to marry her intellectual empowerment, or what she thinks of as her bravery, to her control of her sexuality. The fragility of her level of empowerment indicates both the possibilities of women's resistance to men's pressures and also the depth of critical reflection on their experience which women need in order to become empowered.

The event Sharon initially defined as her first sexual experience was being raped at a school party when she was fourteen.

> Q: When you were first raped did you understand it as rape?
> A: No. I mean I could say now it was a rape, but even still - there's still doubts in my mind. I keep thinking to myself, I was drunk.

She did, however, remember her response in terms of resistance.

> A: ... I can remember screaming, and I can remember someone shouting something - and I can remember him running off ... I can remember running ...

When she was older she had a sexual relationship with a man who physically assaulted her. She left him, then went back to him, even though he had threatened her with a knife and, after escaping again, had been pursued by letters, phone calls and threats. She describes the pressure to have sex in this relationship:

> A: I wouldn't say he was good in bed, or he didn't do anything for me anyway. But there was no night went by without it, because that's the way he wanted it. If I didn't have it he was a total shit.
> Q: Were you able to say what you wanted, that you didn't want to have sex?
> A: If I didn't want to have sex there would have been violence.

Sharon shows that young women can actively resist men's power, even when this power is exercised violently, but their resistance may not necessarily be very effective. Sharon had not just resisted, but had also reflected on her experiences and on what she wanted. In a subsequent relationship she gave an account of herself as much more assertive. She had consciously decided to specify her own needs in the relationship.

> A: Tonight we were supposed to be going out on our own for the evening, and we're not. We're not because he's made different plans. So I turned round and I told him, "OK tonight we'll do what you want, Friday we'll do what I want." So I'm brave enough to do that now...

This progression between pressured sex and empowerment in Sharon's account of her experiences indicates the complexities of understanding empowerment. Towards the end of this interview Sharon mentioned that in the last few months, she had come to recognise that she had been sexually abused as a child, "Oh, the police were involved in it and everything, but I just couldn't admit to myself that it was abuse". This exploration of her past sexuality had altered her understanding of female sexuality.

> Q: Did you expect to enjoy sex at that time?
> A: No, no. Now I'm learning it can be. I've still not found it, but ...! I mean. I know it's possible now to actually enjoy it, you know, and get full pleasure out of it. I've just got to figure out how to do it.

She went on to say that she had never had an orgasm, and that her next step was to get to know her current boyfriend before starting a sexual relationship, in the hope of learning to find pleasure in sex.

> A: ....emotionally I feel like a virgin. I feel like I've yet to experience sex. All I've ever had is the physical side, now I want the emotional side.

We have conceptualised Sharon as both intellectually and experientially empowered at the time of her interview in that she has identified pressure as coming from men and from her own experiences of sexual violence. Far from being a victim, she envisages herself as having agency. How far the changes in her knowledge and expectations will enable her to control future sexual encounters, however, cannot be predicted.

Tina

Tina illustrated a much more assured process of integrating intellectual and experiential levels of empowerment since she had learned that men had to be educated if women were to ensure their own sexual safety and sexual pleasure.

At the time of this interview Tina was 21 years old, living independently from her family and unemployed. She had left home at 18, feeling that she had escaped from a difficult family (her mother died of cervical cancer when she was 15 and her father subsequently remarried) and from a poor working class neighbourhood. She was very aware of the social pressures and constraints of the area in which she grew up. This type of social awareness was matched by a strong assertion of personal agency, a quality which she ascribed to the influence of her mother.

This sense of agency is reflected in her discussion of her experiences of relationships in the past. Her first sexual experience was with another woman, after which she went out with older boys "probably because a lot of boys my age were emotionally immature". However her confidence is matched by an awareness of the way in which power is embedded in many forms of sexual relationships and a willingness to confront this power.

> A: I saw friends, people I know, go out with older blokes and being frightened to say no, or to suggest things - because the bloke would be older. And they didn't feel fully in control of their own bodies - feelings like what was an orgasm? Most women didn't know what they should feel. It was very much on the receiving

side, doing something to please someone else. Not pleasure for themselves. So when it came down to contraception, "Oh I went on the pill to please my boyfriend", because they didn't like sheaths for whatever reason. - They didn't feel in control, as an equal, with the same rights as their boyfriend, because they were younger.

In her contraceptive practice this young woman was a health educator's dream. Her first sexual experience which included intercourse with a man was seen as positive, planned and protected. Using a condom was a "mutual decision". She subsequently went on to the pill while continuing to use condoms. Her sexual practice in her relationships was informed by a shrewd understanding of practical sexual politics and a willingness to engage in confrontation.

A: A lot of men don't actually realise that you do have pleasure out of it. Or that you should. Or they're so engrossed in what they're doing or feeling that you don't come into it at all.

Her experience went beyond confrontation into negotiation over sexual practice in which, unlike Angela who had been afraid of being labelled a prick tease, Tina thought that men should think about what they were doing.

A: In a blackmail situation where a boy's got an erection and he wants to have sexual intercourse with me, I don't. Then I'll talk about it and start laughing. I'll say 'look what you're doing, it's totally unreasonable'. I'll put the funny side on to it. Get them to actually think about what they're doing. Because the majority of men don't think - "well why am I doing this?" There's a lot of people who did things they didn't really want to do. So I'm thinking, well why did they do it? Through thinking about things like that, everyday things, so [now] I can discuss things with people which are of a delicate nature. I've got over it, but I did go through it. I haven't always been able to say "No, no I don't, no I won't."

Tina had been able to integrate the theory and practice of empowerment in an unusually strong way. Such integration relies on both a pragmatic understanding of, and a positive response to the 'masculinist' rules of sexual interaction. By valuing her own sense of self and independence she is able to define her own version of sexual practice. In heterosexual sexual interaction this, by definition, entails engaging with men and a male model of sexual practice.

When asked about her sexual behaviour in the context of HIV/AIDS and safe sex Tina was unusual (in terms of our sample) in distinguishing between condom use and safe sex. She connected sexual safety to her positive expectations of sexual pleasure and her willingness to redefine 'normal' sexual conventions.

> Q: Did you change your behaviour? [because of HIV/AIDS]
> A: Yes I did, not in cutting down the relationships I've had. What I did, I made sure I had sheaths and also safe sex.
> Q: What do you understand as safe sex?
> A: Safe sex is as pleasurable an experience as actual penetration. Oral sex, just things like touching somebody else's body in a very gentle way. Kissing. Appreciating one another's bodies.
> I think it's just as [much] fun, if not more. You concentrate on each others needs a lot more, you're a lot more aware of them. You're aware of each others bodies a lot more.. Instead of 20 minutes of bang, bang bang, you've got a whole night; you watch the dawn come up and you're still there.
> Q: Have you had to convert your partners? Have you come across men who understand sex as being more than penetration?
> A: Yes...I've said, "I don't want to do that", or "why don't you try this?". Before they know it they're converted, and they suddenly realise - "well we haven't actually done it". - "Well I'm tired now, haven't you had a good time?" You can change a lot of people's ideas.

Tina's account indicates something of the possibilities of intellectual/experiential empowerment, even though this is very far from the practice of most young women. The challenge to sex education is now to consider how such practices can be effectively promoted to more conventional young women. Educating young people in positive models of masculine and feminine sexuality while also attempting to transform the model of male sexuality which informs young men's sexual practices is a major social undertaking (Thomson and Scott 1990a).

Conclusion

This small group of relatively empowered young women may not all have been successful in achieving safer sex, but they stand out from the rest of the sample in the extent to which they have reflected on their experience and thought critically about what they do and what has happened to them. This process of critical reflection seems to be an important factor in the struggle for experiential empowerment since effective strategies for safer sex for women necessarily confront the current dominance of men's needs in sexual relationships.

We cannot then think of empowerment as achieving safer sex simply in terms of encouraging more assertive individuals. Empowerment has to be a collective project which shifts the balance of power between women and men throughout society. The examples we have selected show something of the daunting obstacles which face assertive young women who try to put their intellectual empowerment into practice. These obstacles are rooted in women's own conceptions of masculinity and femininity as well as broader social pressures and in men's behaviour. Our five case studies illustrate the ambiguity concerning a woman's rights over her own body within heterosexual sexual culture. However it is these very issues: a woman's sense of ownership of her body, the independence of her sexuality, the conception of desire, that are vital components of intellectual empowerment. If conventions of sexual practice which are 'safe' in the sense of pregnancy, STDs and HIV/AIDS are to be transformed, empowerment must be not only intellectual but also experiential. Intellectually it means women being able to challenge the status quo of heterosexual sexual interaction. In practice it entails personally and generally confronting men with the existence of female desire and the possibilities of a positive female sexuality.

We have conceived young women's empowerment in terms of their ability to change not only their sexual behaviour, but also men's behaviour towards them in developing strategies for safer sex (see also Wellings 1988). In the long term, safe sex must be a set of strategies which women can carry with them between relationships. If young women depend on non-penetrative sex then they have a strategy which is difficult to achieve in practice, but is a form of safer sex which travels with the person rather than being dependent on the context of sexual encounters. Maintaining a sense of personal empowerment which is independent of context and relationship can be difficult and lonely. It requires young women to negotiate a new model of sexuality which treats female sexual pleasure as a priority, and it has not yet been taken seriously by the health education establishment (see also Wilton, 1991).

Since the process of empowerment in the lives of young women constitutes a challenge to male power, being empowered does not mean that young women can provide themselves with total protection in every risky sexual situation. Safer sex for young women constitutes a challenge to the ideas, identities, expectations and practices of men. Empowerment remains a contested process and we recognise the categories of empowerment that we have used as unstable categories. Intellectual/ experiential empowerment, however, does mean the power to recognise the constraints of different sexual situations, to define women's needs and to negotiate choices within these constraints. When young women manage the negotiation of sexual encounters safely it is because they are managing their own lives.

Notes

1. The Women, Risk and AIDS Project is staffed by the authors working collectively, and has been financed by a two year grant from the ESRC. It has also received a small grant from Goldsmiths' College Research Fund. Valuable assistance has been given by Jane Preston, Polly Radcliffe and Janet Ransom. WRAP has used a purposive sample to interview 150 young women aged 16-21 in London and Manchester in depth, and has additional data from 500 questionnaires. The Leverhulme Trust has given a further one year grant for a study of young men, and for comparison of the two studies.

2. The average age at first sexual intercourse of the 22 sexually active young women in the sub-set discussed in this paper was 15.95 years. In the sample as a whole the average age was 15.4 years: for middle class young women the average was 16.27 years; for working class young women it was 14.49 years.

3. Analysis of the ways in which this sub-set of young women respond to male violence in sexual relationships, and how these responses may be related to empowerment, is dealt with in Holland et al. 1991b.

4. For discussion of the theory of rational choice see Hindess 1988. The use of this model in HIV/AIDS health promotion has been criticised by Watney (1990).

5. Kate and Rachel Thomson in discussion.

6. A systemic network is an analytic device suitable for the organisation and categorisation of qualitative data, preserving and representing some of the original essence of these data. A network is an instrument for enabling theory to be tested, translating the language of, in this instance, the interview transcript into the language of the theory. This helps with the interpretation of the patterns and meanings in the data (Bliss et al. 1983). The conceptual categories constituting the network can be derived exclusively from theoretical concepts, but in this case came from developing interaction between feminist and sociological theory, the responses of the subjects and the researchers' experiences of the interviews.

7. For further discussion of methods see Thomson and Scott (1990) and Ramazanoglu (1990).

8. The names of the young women interviewed and of their partners have been changed to preserve confidentiality.

References

Azjen, I. and Fishbein, M. (1980) *Understanding Attitudes and Predicting Social Behaviour* New York, Prentice-Hall.

Bliss, J., Monk, M., and Ogborn, J. (1983) *Qualitative data analysis for educational research*, London, Croom Helm.

Christophers, H. (1990) *AIDS Dialogue* 8:5-7.

Coward, R. (1987) 'Sex after AIDS' *The New Internationalist* March.

Estaugh, V. and Wheatley, J. (1990) *Family Planning and Family Well-being* London, Family Policy Studies Centre.

Freeman, R. and Scott, S. 'AIDS and prevention' (unpublished).

Gross, A.E. and Bellew-Smith, M. (1983) 'A social psychological approach to reducing pregnancy risk in adolescence' In D. Byrne and W.A. Fisher (eds) *Adolescence, Sex and Contraception* New Jersey, Laurence Erlbaum Associates.

Hanmer, J. and Maynard, M. (1987) *Women, Violence and Social Control* London, Macmillan.

Hanson, S.l., Myers, D.E. and Ginsburg, A.L. (1987) 'The role of responsibility and knowledge in reducing out of wedlock childbearing' *Journal of Marriage and the Family* 49:241-256.

Hindess, B. (1988) *Choice, Rationality and Social Theory* London, Unwin Hyman.

Holland, J., Ramazanoglu, C., Scott, S., Sharpe, S. and Thomson, R. (1991a) 'Between embarrassment and trust: Young women and the diversity of condom use' in P. Aggleton et al. *AIDS: Responses, Interventions and Care* Brighton, Falmer.

Holland, J., Ramazanoglu, C., Sharpe, S. and Thomson, R. (1991b) 'Pressured pleasure: young women and the negotiation of sexual boundaries' paper delivered to the *Annual Conference of the British Sociological Association,* Manchester, March.

Hunt, S.M. and Macleod, M. 'Health and behavioural change: some lay perspectives' *Community Medicine* 9, 1:68-76.

Jessop, L. and Thorogood, N. (1989) 'The sociology of a sex education project', paper presented to the *British Sociological Association Annual Conference,* Plymouth.

Kelly, L. (1988) *Surviving Sexual Violence* Cambridge, Polity.

Kent, V., Davies, M., Deverell, K. and Gottesman, S. (1990) 'Social interaction routines involved in heterosexual encounters: prelude to first intercourse'. Paper presented at the *Fourth Conference on the Social Aspects of AIDS* London.

Office of Population Censuses and Surveys (1991) *OPCS Monitor* PP2 91/1, London, OPCS.

Ramazanoglu, C. (1990) *Methods of Working as a Research Team* WRAP paper 3, London, the Tufnell Press.

Raven, B.H. and Litman-Adizes, T. (1986) 'Interpersonal influence and social power in health promotion' In T.Z. Salisbury *et al.* (eds) *Advances in Health Education and Promotion* Vol I. Jai Press.

Rumbold, J. (1991) 'Goodbye to all that' *The Guardian* 13th March.

Setters, J. (1988) 'Safer sex guidelines for heterosexuals' *Health Education Journal* 47, 3 & 4:61-2.

Stanko, E. (1985) *Intimate Intrusions: Women's Experience of Male Violence* London, RKP.

Thomson, R. and Scott, S. (1990a) *Learning about Sex: Young women and the social construction of sexual identity* WRAP paper 4, London, the Tufnell Press

Thomson, R. and Scott, S. (1990b) *Researching Sexuality in the light of AIDS: Historical and methodological issues* WRAP paper 5, London, the Tufnell Press.

Thompson, S. (1984) 'Searching for tomorrow: on feminism and the reconstruction of teen romance' in C. Vance (ed.) *Pleasure and Danger: Exploring Female Sexuality* London, RKP.

Watney, S. (1990) 'Plenary Session' *Fourth Conference on the Social Aspects of AIDS* London.

Wellings, K. (1988) 'Do we need to change sexual behaviour, should we, can we? *Health Education Journal* 47, 3 & 4:57-60.

Williams, D. (1990) 'Interview with Mukesh Kapila' *AIDS Dialogue* 8:3-4.

Wilton, T. (1990) 'Condoms, coercion and control: AIDS and heterosexual practice' *Fourth Conference on the Social Aspects of AIDS* London.

Wilton, T. (1991) 'Feminism and the erotics of health promotion' paper given at the Fifth Conference on the Social Aspects of AIDS, London.

Appendix

The Empowerment Network

An empirically based model of women's empowerment in relation to sexuality, sexual encounters and relationships

We have defined empowerment operationally for this exercise as: *ways in which, and routes through which, young women can attempt to, or do take control over their own sexual activity and/or relationships*.

The network is an attempt to draw a conceptual map of women's experiences of empowerment and disempowerment. We have tried also to indicate process in the network. The downward arrow indicates recursivity, in that the categories which follow are not mutually exclusive, and you can go into this part of the network as many times as it takes to categorise and describe the datum, text or unit of experience adequately. The bracket indicates that the categories which follow should be co-selected. Individuals may for example be *experientially* or *intellectually* empowered, but it is most likely that there are elements of each. The concept of *'experiential and intellectual'* outlines possible directions and outcomes and should be used in relation to the *'experiential'* and *'intellectual'* categories.

From our data, we can see that empowerment is not a once and for all attainment, but a process, and a struggle. A crucial category then is the *transitional* category which captures the contingent nature of empowerment in practice. It indicates the effects of gendered power relations, realised in the sexual encounter through male power over young women's ability to experience and exert their own power.

We can cross-cut our data on the sub-set of 26 young women whom we have identified as demonstrating empowerment to illustrate the categories of the network as they realise the data. But since process is crucial to the understanding of, as well as to the actualisation of, the possibilities of empowerment, the selection of case-studies which can illustrate the processes through which individual young women attain, lose, regain empowerment was considered appropriate for this paper.

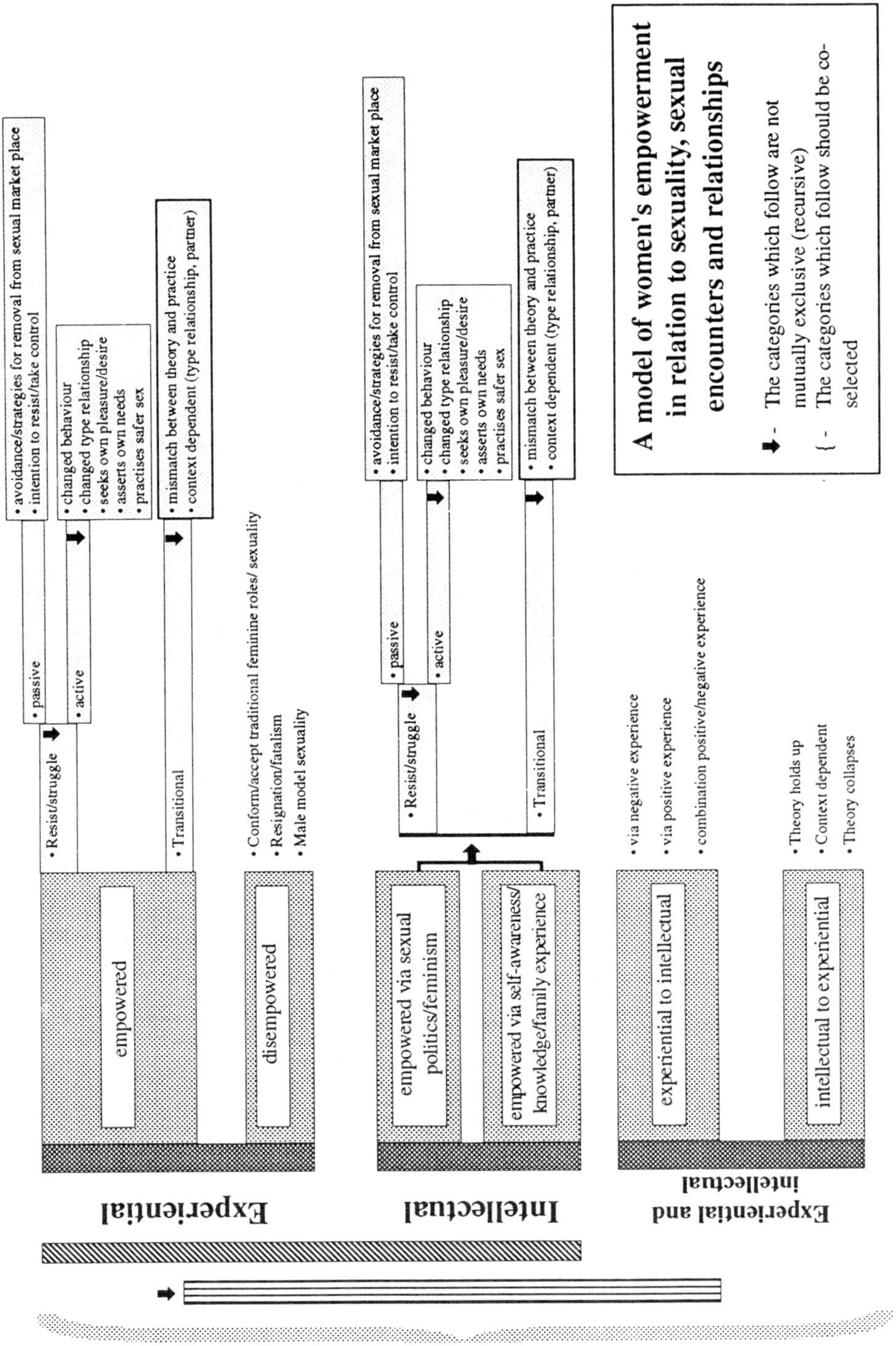
A model of women's empowerment in relation to sexuality, sexual encounters and relationships
➡ - The categories which follow are not mutually exclusive (recursive)
{ - The categories which follow should be co-selected
Experiential
empowered
• Resist/struggle
• passive
• avoidance/strategies for removal from sexual market place
• intention to resist/take control
• active
• changed behaviour
• changed type relationship
• seeks own pleasure/desire
• asserts own needs
• practises safer sex
• Transitional
• mismatch between theory and practice
• context dependent (type relationship, partner)
disempowered
• Conform/accept traditional feminine roles/ sexuality
• Resignation/fatalism
• Male model sexuality
Intellectual
empowered via sexual politics/feminism
empowered via self-awareness/ knowledge/family experience
• Resist/struggle
• passive
• avoidance/strategies for removal from sexual market place
• intention to resist/take control
• active
• changed behaviour
• changed type relationship
• seeks own pleasure/desire
• asserts own needs
• practises safer sex
• Transitional
• mismatch between theory and practice
• context dependent (type relationship, partner)
Experiential and intellectual
experiential to intellectual
• via negative experience
• via positive experience
• combination positive/negative experience
intellectual to experiential
• Theory holds up
• Context dependent
• Theory collapses

WRAP Publications

Wimp or gladiator: Contradictions in acquiring masculine sexuality

Janet Holland, Caroline Ramazanoglu, & Sue Sharpe

As young men struggle to attain masculinity, they are drawn into the exercise of power over women, but at the same time exposed to the possibilities of failure. Using depth interviews with young men aged 16-21, in this paper we explore their strategies for defending themselves against vulnerability in the process of acquiring heterosexual masculinity. These strategies include adopting the protective coloration of the peer group, impugning a woman's reputation, objectifying women (the 'bastard' syndrome), and seeking out the sexually knowing older woman. Without young men necessarily intending that this should be so, these strategies reproduce and reinforce the exercise of male power over women. We trace the operation of these strategies in the young men's accounts of their own experiences.

210 x 150 mm	*40pp*	*1993*
ISBN 1 872767 90 7	*Paperback*	*£3.50*

Sexuality and ethnicity: Variations in young women's sexual knowledge and practice

Janet Holland

In this paper the author describes the sample of 150 young women who took part in the WRAP study, focusing on similarities and differences between young women from different broad ethnic groups - white, African-Caribbean, and Asian. We discuss their experience and knowledge of sex education, AIDS and AIDS education, and consider family and cultural influences on sexual behaviour. Their perceptions of men, women and sexual relationships, and understanding of risk and safety in sexual encounters are examined. Despite differences in class, cultural, religious and educational background there was perhaps a surprising degree of similarity in the young women's responses. The paper concludes by drawing out implications of the findings for policy and practice.

210 x 150 mm	*44pp*	*1993*
ISBN 1 872767 85 0	*Paperback*	*£3.50*

Pressured pleasure: Young women and the negotiation of sexual boundaries

Janet Holland, Caroline Ramazanoglu, Sue Sharpe & Rachel Thomson

Women develop and live their sexuality through an interrelated range of pressures; personal, social, physical. The authors examine the continuum of pressure, from social expectation to male physical violence, which shapes women's sexuality, sexual identity and sexual health. They describe and illustrate the boundaries of sexual pressure and violence, and the degree to which women are able to negotiate these boundaries. Modes of resistance and types of experience, both negative and positive, which can enable young women to take control over their own sexuality and sexual experienceare examined.

210 x 150 mm | *30pp* | *1992*
ISBN 1 872767 80 X | *Paperback* | *£3.50*

Pressure, resistance, empowerment: Young women and the negotiation of safer sex

Janet Holland, Caroline Ramazanoglu, Sue Scott, Sue Sharpe & Rachel Thomson

We reflect here on the sexual politics of safer sex by considering ways in which young women can become empowered in sexual encounters. Selected case studies illustrate difficulties which young women face in taking control of their sexuality and sexual experience. Some become assertive individuals, but their experiences demonstrate that empowerment for women must be a collective project shifting the balance of power between men and women throughout society.

210 x 150 mm | *30pp* | *1991*
ISBN 1 872767 75 3 | *Paperback* | *£3.00*

Learning about sex: young women and the social construction of sexual identity

Rachel Thomson & Sue Scott

Sex education is an interactive process in which young women actively engage with, resist and accommodate a range of contradictory messages and models. In this paper the way young women experience 'learning about sex' related to their sexual practice and expectations of sexual pleasure is examined. Available models of female sexuality and influences and information sources including the home, peer groups, popular culture and experience are discussed. Understanding the social construction of sexual identity has important implications for the negotiation of safe sex.

210 X 150 mm | *55 pp* | *1992 (rev)*
ISBN 1 872767 70 2 | *Paperback* | *£3.50*

'Don't die of ignorance' - I nearly died of embarrassment: Condoms in context

Janet Holland, Caroline Ramazanoglu, Sue Scott, Sue Sharpe, and Rachel Thomson

Negotiation of sexual encounters is a complex process with many different outcomes. In this paper the relationship between knowledge of risk and safer sex practices is examined through an analysis of young women's reported experience of condom use, from which it is clear that gendered power relations construct and constrain the choices open to young women.

210 X 150 mm | *30 pp* | *1990*
ISBN 1 872767 50 8 | *Paperback* | *£3.00*

Sex, risk and danger: AIDS education policy and young women's sexuality

Janet Holland, Caroline Ramazanoglu and Sue Scott

The authors review the history of the AIDS epidemic in medical science, social research and public policy, highlighting the way in which women have been perceived and represented in that process. AIDS education aimed at young heterosexuals is evaluated in the light of the findings of an investigation of the sexual knowledge and practice of a group of young women.

210 X 150 mm	*30 pp*	*1990*
ISBN 1 872767 55 9	*Paperback*	*£3.00*

Researching sexuality in the light of AIDS: Historical and methodological issues

Rachel Thomson and Sue Scott

The methodological implications of treating sexuality as a socially constructed subject are explored in relation to the findings of the WRAP study of young women's sexuality.

210 X 150 mm	*26 pp*	*1990*
ISBN 1 872767 65 6	*Paperback*	*£3.00*

Methods of working as a research team

Caroline Ramazanoglu

The author examines problems of making explicit the relationship between theory construction and data production; of hierarchical relationships within the team; of power in the research process; of the negotiation of meanings both with informants and within the research team; of validity and interpretation of qualitative data; and of the place of trust and emotion in the research process.

210 X 150 mm	*30 pp*	*1990*
ISBN 1 872767 60 5	*Paperback*	*£3.00*

the Tufnell Press
47 Dalmeny Road,
London, N7 ODY

ORDER FORM

Please send me the following:

	Price	Quantity	Total

Total amount enclosed ______

Please make cheques payable to the Tufnell Press

NAME ______________________

ADDRESS ______________________

____

____

W6/1993